ACOLYTE HANDBOOK

PRESENTED TO

_____

by

_____

_____, *Pastor*

Date _____

D1417474

ACOLYTE
HANDBOOK
Ralph R. Van Loon

FORTRESS PRESS   PHILADELPHIA

Illustrations by Barbara Churchville.
Illustration on p. 17 courtesy of Carlton Gross.

COPYRIGHT © 1987 BY FORTRESS PRESS

All rights reserved. No part of this publication may be reproduced, stored in a retrieval system, or transmitted in any form or by any means, electronic, mechanical, photocopying, recording, or otherwise, without the prior permission of the publisher, Fortress Press.

———————

Library of Congress Cataloging-in-Publication Data

Van Loon, Ralph R.
  Acolyte handbook.

    1. Acolytes—Lutheran Church—Handbooks, manuals, etc. 2. Lutheran Church—Liturgy—Handbooks, manuals, etc. I. Title.
BX8067.A68V36   1987   264'.041   86–46430
ISBN 0–8006–2059–3

———————

Printed in the United States of America   1-2059

To the altar guilds and acolytes of
Our Saviour's Lutheran Church of Cedar, Minnesota
Concordia Lutheran Church of Duluth, Minnesota

Contents

Introduction

Congratulations!

Something exciting is happening to you. You have been asked to serve as an acolyte—that makes you a special kind of minister. No, you are not a pastor, at least not yet. And becoming an acolyte doesn't mean that you are being ordained. And yet, to be an acolyte is to be a minister, for you will be serving at the altar of God, handling holy things, assisting the pastor, and helping everyone at church see something of the goodness and glory of God when they come to worship.

All of us have gifts; being able to do some particular task particularly well means that God has blessed us in a special way. It also means that God expects us to take good care of those gifts—working with them, improving our use of them, and knowing that each gift is really to be used for the good of others and for the glory of God.

All of us have gifts, and that includes you. Since you are now studying to be a good acolyte, you probably have some special gifts that will help you become a good minister at God's altar. That kind of minister knows how to act liturgically, how to handle holy things, how to help the people worship, and how to help the people see something of the majesty of God.

Wanting to be a good acolyte is probably a sign that you have the gifts to become a good acolyte. You need to know, however, that such gifts need to have the chance to grow and to be developed. That means learning as much as you can about the things acolytes are expected to do at worship. There's a new vocabulary to learn if you are going to be a good acolyte; words like *liturgy, chancel, chalice, credence table.* But you're used to that; you're always learning new words. If someone is going to be a good tennis player, it is necessary to understand such words as *set, racket, love, deuce, ad.* Trying to play tennis without knowing such a basic vocabulary may make it difficult to take the game seriously. Or when one is learning to drive a car, it is necessary to understand such words as *ignition, gearshift, brake.* Trying to pass a driving test without knowing such a basic vocabulary means that you won't get a driver's license.

Good tennis players and good drivers always know and understand their basic vocabulary. Good acolytes will do the same thing. After all, if the pastor asks one of the acolytes to put the lectionary on the credence table, who will understand the acolyte's decision to put a chasuble in the font? A good acolyte would not make such a mistake; a good acolyte will take the time to learn the words and terms that have to do with the worship life of the church. Don't worry—you won't have to learn all those words and terms all at once, nor will you have to learn all at once everything that an acolyte does at all of the many services of the church. It takes time to become a good acolyte; this handbook asks that you be willing to take that time.

As you continue your training to be an acolyte, you need to remember that each congregation has its own way of doing things. Some congregations have several candles on the altar and some have only two. Some congregations have processions every Sunday and some have them only a few times a year. Some congregations use incense and some do not. Some have Holy Communion every Sunday and others celebrate that sacrament less often. As you study this handbook and as you prepare to be an acolyte in your congregation, you will need to find out what your pastor expects of you and to serve as he or she asks.

1
What
Is an
Acolyte ?

A long time ago, the church decided that pastors should be assisted by specially trained persons when Christians gathered to worship. As early as the fourth century, pastors were being assisted by persons who had such titles as deacons, subdeacons, cantors, readers, and doorkeepers. Not long after that came acolytes—persons trained to carry the cross and candles and incense in procession and to assist the other worship leaders during the service. Some say that acolytes have an even longer history—that Samuel, who assisted Eli in the Old Testament temple, was really the first acolyte.

The word *acolyte* means "follower" or "attendant." In the early days of the church, serving as an acolyte was one of the steps toward becoming a pastor. In this way, future pastors would get to learn all about Christian worship—what it means, how it should be led, and how important those moments are to the church and to all who attend. In those early years, acolytes who did their tasks well would become subdeacons and, if they served well, they could eventually become deacons. As deacons, they were permitted to lead certain parts of the service and could look forward to being ordained as pastors. When that happened, they would be given the privilege of leading the liturgy, standing at the altar in the footsteps of Christ Jesus.

There have been many changes in the church since then. Today no one expects every acolyte to become a pastor, although most pastors probably served as acolytes in their younger years. What has not changed is the need for such worship assistants. It's not because pastors are overworked every Sunday. It's because worship is a group event, where all come together offering their gifts and talents and skills and abilities in the praise of God. Acolytes are needed because their learnings and skills as worship leaders are needed. Acolytes are needed because they have a special ministry to perform at each service. Acolytes are needed to:

help get the church ready for worship

know what's supposed to happen and help it happen

do their tasks with reverence and care

make it obvious that worship is a holy event

let every word and action declare the glory of God

let a deep love for God and God's holy church be always apparent during worship

put everything in place following the service

live out their Baptism throughout the week

Acolytes are, therefore, ministers of the church. They are much more than just candle lighters and offering receivers. They are part of a long tradition in the Christian church, bringing to each celebration of the liturgy a necessary and useful and special ministry. That's a tradition worth protecting and preserving. It's a ministry that deserves careful preparation and the acolyte's very best efforts. As such, good acolytes hate all forms of sloppiness and carelessness. They know that God is being served at worship and that God should not have to put up with anything less than the best:

acolytes want worshipers to notice God—not them

acolytes will make sure that their appearance is neat and clean

hair will be combed and nails will be clean

shoes will be polished; sneakers will stay home

faces will be scrubbed and so will hands

jewelry will be out of sight or left at home

acolytes won't scratch, yawn, slouch, chew gum, or fidget

acolytes will be fully involved in each part of the service

After all, acolytes are ministers. They are part of a tradition that reaches back to the early years of Christianity and that has had but one aim: to give praise to God and to help worshipers to see something of the goodness and glory of God.

2
What
Is the
Liturgy ?

For Christians, nothing is more important than the time we spend at worship. Ever since God gave the Commandments to Moses, we've understood that worship is a necessary part of the religious life and that God does not want any of us to face a week without it. During the days of the New Testament, Jesus went to worship every week, giving us the model for our lives and making it clear that regular worship is an important part of the Christian life.

Before Christ was born, the people of God worshiped in the Temple in Jerusalem or in neighborhood centers called synagogues. In the Temple, complicated sacrifices (including the killing of certain animals) were performed by the priests to praise God or to seek God's favor or forgiveness. In the synagogues, where worship was much more informal and simple, the emphasis was on the hearing of the Word of God and on prayer.

Worship for the people of God changed considerably as a result of the ministry of Jesus the Savior. As the sacrificial Lamb of God, Jesus went to the cross and was there slaughtered for the sins of all people. To make it absolutely clear that his death on the cross could change everything and everyone everywhere, Jesus rose triumphantly from the grave three days later on the Sunday we call Easter.

The birth, ministry, death, and resurrection of Jesus changed forever the worship life of the people of God. In fact, Jesus gave Christians their new order of worship the night he was betrayed. That new order for worship, shared with the disciples during the Last Supper in the Upper Room, had four basic elements:

thanksgiving to God
blessing and giving of the bread as the Body of Christ

blessing and giving of the cup of wine as the Blood of Christ
—all done in remembrance of the saving acts of God

For several years after the ascension of Jesus to heaven, Christians continued going to the Temple and to synagogues but they also gathered together to repeat the words and actions of the Upper Room—the Holy Communion. One of the apostles, or someone appointed by the apostles, took the place of Jesus at each celebration of that service, doing and saying what Jesus had said and done in the Upper Room when the Holy Communion was instituted.

Later, Christians began to add the synagogue service to the Upper Room service, and that is how Christian worship took on the shape that it still has today. From the synagogue has come the first half of the Christian service, called the *Liturgy of the Word*. During this part of the service we pay attention to God's Word as it is read, sung, preached, and confessed. From the Upper Room has come the second half of the Christian service, called the *Liturgy of the Eucharistic Meal*. During this part of the service we recall and celebrate the death and resurrection of Christ Jesus and, in thankful remembrance, share in the eating and drinking of the Lord's Supper.

For Christians, the celebration of the full liturgy of Word and Meal is a time of great holiness. It is that time when God is present in a special and awesome way, coming with angels and archangels to be with us. Through this liturgy of Word and Meal several things happen:

the baptized gather before God's throne on earth, the altar

carefully and solemnly, God's saving acts are recalled

believers are given instruction and encouragement from God's Word

through prayers for each other and the world, God's will, love, and peace are sought

carefully and solemnly, believers retrace what happened to Jesus during the days of Holy Week

with thanksgiving, believers accept the gift of the crucified and risen Christ—his own Body and Blood, given and shed for us because he loves us and desires to be with us always, even to the end of the world

forgiven, remade, and renewed, believers then go to do ministry in their homes, schools, and work places

To be a part of this God-event is no small matter. To have a leadership assignment at this God-event can't help but be a bit overwhelming. Acolyte, reader, singer, presiding minister—we're all being used by God so that several helpful things can happen to the people of God every time they gather for the liturgy of the Word and the Meal. What you do as an acolyte at that liturgy is of great importance. You must always keep in mind that at worship earth becomes connected to heaven, believers are permitted to gain a glimpse of the majesty and glory of God, the whole church on earth joins with the whole church in heaven to praise God, and no believer is ever quite the same again.

Please understand: at worship we are in the presence of the most high God. Whether we light one candle or two hundred, whether we carry a cross or a cruet, we are at service before the throne of almighty God. The sincere praise of God is our only assignment. With this understanding of worship, acolytes and other worship leaders will prepare carefully for each service and will serve with care, humility, reverence, and awe.

3
Where
Does the
Liturgy Happen ?

For about the first three hundred years of Christianity, believers were treated as outlaws and enemies by the government of the Roman Empire. During those difficult centuries, Christians were forced to worship in secret. If they were discovered doing liturgy, the government of Rome would punish them; many of our spiritual ancestors were killed because they would not stop their celebrations of Holy Communion. Christians had no church buildings in those days. Instead, believers gathered in private homes, in caves, out in the country, or sometimes even in graveyards to worship.

In the year 313 all of this changed. The emperor Constantine not only made Christianity legal that year, he made it the favored religion of the Roman Empire. To make up for some of the sufferings Christians had endured, the emperor gave the church many large and beautiful public buildings as places for worship. Those buildings were usually rectangular, having been designed for use as courthouses and public markets. The Christians found that such buildings worked very well for the liturgy, and we often plan buildings like those when we design churches today.

Through the centuries, Christians have made some decisions about their places of worship—how they should be designed and furnished. While no two church buildings in the world are exactly alike, most are very similar in room design and furnishings: we always need a place to gather and we always need certain furnishings for the liturgy.

This chapter is about those places and those pieces. A good acolyte needs to be well acquainted with both, for they represent where acolytes do their serving and the furnishings with which they work.

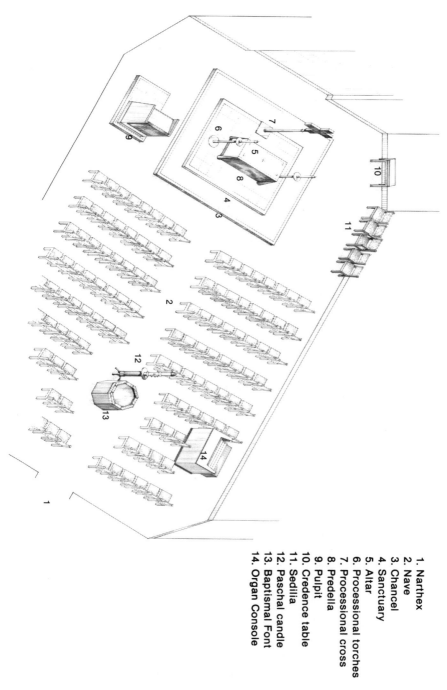

1. Narthex
2. Nave
3. Chancel
4. Sanctuary
5. Altar
6. Processional torches
7. Processional cross
8. Predella
9. Pulpit
10. Credence table
11. Sedilia
12. Paschal candle
13. Baptismal Font
14. Organ Console

THE CHURCH BUILDING

Most church buildings have three rooms (narthex, nave, sacristy) and two special areas (chancel and sanctuary). Because these are the rooms and areas in which acolytes do their serving, these spaces should be familiar to them:

Narthex

Narthex is the room that serves as the entryway into the worship space. In other buildings, this room would be called a lobby or a vestibule. The narthex is a kind of "decompression chamber" for worshipers; it's the place where worldly distractions are put aside and thoughts are directed toward the liturgy that is about to happen. The narthex is also worship space since processions may form there for entry into the room where the believers have gathered.

Nave

Nave is the room where the believers gather to do liturgy. The nave may have pews for seating people, or it may have chairs. The windows in the nave may be of colored glass, perhaps depicting stories from the Bible or church history. Naves usually have a central aisle that leads toward the altar, as well as side aisles; all aisles provide passageways for liturgical processions.

The nave of the church is not a kind of auditorium, where people gather to watch and listen. All believers are expected to be fully involved in the action of the liturgy. Liturgy is, after all, something that we *do;* it's an action event.

Chancel

Chancel is an area in the worship space; it includes everything in front of the nave. In the chancel are spaces such as the sanctuary and furnishings such as the altar, pulpit, and sedilia.

Sanctuary

Sanctuary is the name of the most prominent and most significant space in the building; it's where the altar is located. Since the word *sanctuary* means "holy place," it is easy to understand why the church saves such a word for that special and holy spot that houses the altar.

Sacristy

Sacristy is a room in the church that is very important to acolytes and other worship leaders. In some churches, there may be more than one sacristy, one for the altar guild and one for the putting on of vestments. The sacristy is the place where all the vestments, paraments, sacramental vessels, and linens are kept. The sacristy is a busy room, for this is where the altar guild prepares everything for every service. This is where linens, vestments, and vessels are brought after each service for proper cleaning and storage.

THE FURNISHINGS OF THE CHURCH

Christians have a need for several items as they do liturgy. It is helpful to remember that Christian liturgy began at a table, with food, with cups and plates, and with places to sit. Because we always try as much as possible to be faithful to Christ's way of doing the liturgy, we still use such items in our worship today. Each of these items has its own name; it is important that acolytes know these items—their names, their uses, what they look like, where they are stored, and where they should be placed during the service.

Altar

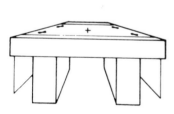

This is the most important object in the church. It is the place where we celebrate the Holy Communion. It is the "table of the Lord." The word *altar* means "high place." In our church buildings, the altar is positioned so that all worshipers can see it, and it is constructed and adorned so that all may know that no other furnishing can match its importance.

An altar may take the shape of a table. The fact that Jesus was at a table when he instituted the Holy Communion helps us understand why a table is still used in many of our churches. During the early years of Christianity before we had church buildings, believers gathered around the family table in private homes when they celebrated the Lord's Supper.

Some altars are shaped as a long, oblong box. This is known as a "tomb altar." Many centuries ago, during those early years of Christianity when believers were killed if they were caught at worship, the graves of those who died for the faith were regarded as holy places. Their tombs were used as altars, as places to celebrate the Holy Communion.

• The top surface of every altar is called a **mensa.** It is quite common to find five crosses carved into the mensa: one in the middle and one at each corner. These five crosses remind us of the five wounds of Jesus on the cross—one in each hand and foot, and the one in his side.

• Historically, the two ends of the altar are referred to as **horns:** the Epistle horn and the Gospel horn. It was once the custom to read the Epistle lesson from the right end of the altar and to read the Gospel from the left. Altars are still described as having an Epistle side (on the right as you face the altar) and a Gospel side (on the left as you face the altar). Knowing these terms is especially useful since pastors often give directions to acolytes about placing something on the Epistle or Gospel end of the altar.

Altar Candles

At least two candles are on or beside every altar. Candles always remind us of Jesus the Light of the World and of those dangerous days when Christians had to huddle in secret around a dimly lighted table or a tomb to celebrate Holy Communion.

Altar Cloths

Two linens are on the altar at all times:

Cerecloth (SAIR-cloth), placed directly upon the mensa

Fair Linen, placed on top of the cerecloth, its ends covering the sides of the altar

During the celebration of Holy Communion, these linens are also used at the altar:

Corporal, a square cloth, placed in the middle of the mensa, on which the sacramental vessels are set

Pall, a small, stiff, linen-covered square that is set upon the chalice (Communion cup)

Purificators, small linen napkins used to cleanse the chalice

Chalice Veil, a covering for the chalice and pall

Burse, a fabric-covered "envelope" for the corporal

Paraments

These are fabric coverings for the front of the altar and pulpit. Their color is determined by the season or day of the church year.

Sacramental Vessels

These are the "dinner pieces" used to serve the Lord's Supper:

Chalice (CHAL-us), the metal or ceramic cup that holds the wine to be distributed during Communion

Paten, the plate that holds the bread to be distributed during Communion

Ciborium (sih-BOR-ee-um), looks like a chalice, although it has a lid; contains wafers for the Holy Communion

Host Box, a container used to store Communion wafers

Cruet, a small pitcher used for pouring wine into the chalice

Flagon, a large pitcher used for pouring wine into the chalice

Lavabo (lah-VAH-boe), a small basin used to cleanse the fingers of the presiding minister

Communion Tray, a container for small individual glasses sometimes used to serve the wine for Communion

Missal Stand

 This book holder is placed on the mensa just before the liturgy begins and is removed from the altar following each service. The book (missal) that it holds is the altar book, the ministers' edition.

Baptismal Font

This large vessel or pool contains the water that is used for the Sacrament of Holy Baptism.

Baptistery

The baptistery is the name given to that section of the worship space where the baptismal font is located.

Paschal Candle

This tall, white candle stands in a tall holder and is a symbol of Easter, of Baptism, and of the new life. From the Vigil of Easter until Pentecost, it stands lighted near the Gospel end of the altar. At other times, the paschal candle stands near the baptismal font and is lighted for each Baptism. At funeral services, this candle is carried before the coffin as it is brought into the nave and it is then placed at the head of the coffin during the service.

Baptismal Items

Water, of course, is the main element in the baptismal service since Holy Baptism is a bath, a washing away of sin. Other items are also used for this service that help to state clearly the meaning of this sacrament:

Baptismal Oil is used as the presiding minister traces the sign of the cross upon the newly baptized.

Baptismal Garment is the name of the white vestment that is placed on the newly baptized.

Baptismal Candle, lighted from the paschal candle, is presented to the newly baptized during the service.

Sedilia

It is customary to provide special seating for the presiding minister, the one who leads the liturgy as the representative of Christ. The sedilia (suh-DEE-lee-yah) is the name of such seating, and usually includes space for two additional worship leaders. The presiding minister is always seated in the middle space of the sedilia.

Credence Table

This is also called the **credence shelf.** Situated near the altar is a small table or shelf that holds the sacramental vessels and linens until they are brought to the altar.

Offertory Table

A small table, set in the middle aisle near the narthex, holds the bread and wine until they are brought forward to the altar during the Offertory.

Communion Rail

Sometimes called the **altar rail,** it is the place where the people stand or kneel to receive Communion.

Predella

The predella is the platform on which the altar stands.

Pulpit

This furnishing is the "place of the Word," where the Gospel is announced and read, and where the Sermon is preached. The pulpit is sometimes called the **ambo.**

Lectern

In some church buildings, this furnishing is placed in the chancel opposite the pulpit and is sometimes used for reading Lessons.

Lectionary

This is a book which contains the readings assigned for each Sunday and holy day of the church year. This book is sometimes carried in procession by one of the lectors or by an acolyte.

Thurible

This vessel holds the burning incense. Sometimes it is called a **censer.** A special kind of charcoal is used in this vessel to burn the incense. The one who carries the thurible is called the thurifer.

Incense Boat

This vessel holds the incense until it is spooned into the thurible.

Processional Cross

This is a special cross on a tall staff so that all may see and turn toward the cross when it is carried in procession. The one who carries this cross is called the crucifer.

Processional Torches

These are special candles on tall staffs that accompany and illuminate the processional cross. Those who carry such special candles are called torchbearers.

Processional Banners

This is a decorated fabric attached to a tall staff carried in festival processions. Bannerbearer is the title for the one carrying this item in a procession.

Aumbry

The aumbry is a small cupboard in the chancel wall or in the sacristy in which consecrated bread and wine are kept.

Piscina

This is a special basin in the sacristy that drains directly into the ground. Into the piscina (puh-SEE-nah) may be poured the water used for Baptism and any consecrated wine that remains after the celebration of Holy Communion; this avoids the use of the sewer and permits the return of these elements directly to the earth.

Candlelighter and Extinguisher

This is the basic tool for all acolytes. It is a long staff with two prongs. One prong contains a wick to be used when lighting candles. The other prong has a bell-shaped snuffer to extinguish candles by robbing them of oxygen.

Yes, it is a long list. It may be that your church does not have every item mentioned above. If that is the case, mark only those that you use in your church and learn only those.

At the same time, it is necessary to remember that your church may use several items that have not been mentioned. Your pastor will list those for you and describe each of them.

4
What
Do Worship
Leaders Wear?

This chapter is about those special items of clothing that worship leaders wear during the celebration of the liturgy. What are now called "special" were, originally, quite ordinary for the early Christian. In many ways, when our ministers get all dressed up for the liturgy, wearing those long and sometimes very colorful garments, they are just wearing what the early believers wore for everyday. There is no place in the Bible that commands our ministers to dress the way they do, but we would probably be very surprised and even disappointed if our pastors would preside at the altar dressed in a jogging suit. For a very long time, the church has felt that the liturgy deserves something better.

In the Old Testament, God was very specific about the clothing the priests were to wear during Temple services. It was the law that they wear the garments God had named. No such law appears in the New Testament, for Christ came to us with a new set of promises—not a new set of laws.

After the ascension of Jesus, when the apostles and those they ordained presided at Holy Communion, they wore their usual everyday clothes—usually a long, ankle-length garment and, if the weather demanded, they would also wear a kind of poncho. However, one of the earliest set of directives given to pastors by the church was the expectation that whatever clothes they wore when they led the liturgy, those clothes must be clean and neat.

Some pastors began to reserve a set of clothes to be used only for the liturgy. Marking those Sunday clothes with crosses and other Christian symbols became commonplace.

Then fashions began to change and pastors wondered if they should get rid of those long garments and start wearing the new, short ones that everybody else seemed to be buying. The church thought better of it and decided that it is to our advantage to keep wearing the kind of clothing that Jesus and the apostles wore. It was another way to maintain a link with our holy beginnings.

That's one of the reasons that worship leaders dress the way they do. Those items of liturgical clothing are convincing reminders that our roots extend to the very ancient days. But there are other reasons for wearing such garments, called vestments. As the ministers put on these special clothes, they are immediately reminded of the task that is before them; they help them shift their mental gears, discarding all thoughts but those that center on the praise of God and the enrichment of the people of God.

When worshipers see the vested worship leaders, their own thoughts become more focused. Seeing the assisting minister, for example, in alb and cincture permits worshipers to see beyond the person (Alfred Jones, the mechanic; or Mildred Casey, the piano teacher) and see one who is assisting in the proclamation and celebration of the Gospel. Such vestments remind us of our baptismal garments. Then, too, these vestments remind us of the way the saints are dressed who now circle the throne of God in heaven, and they also remind us that we will be dressed like them when we reach our home in heaven.

There are several kinds of vestments in the church. Some may be worn by both pastors and laypersons. Some are to be worn only by pastors. Some are to be worn only for certain services. Some have colors that are to be saved for certain days and seasons of the church year.

Some of this information needs to be clear in your mind. It would not be a good idea for you to go to the pastor's vestment closet and wear whatever looks good to you as you light the candles!

VESTMENTS FOR THE
PRESIDING MINISTER

Two reminders are in order: (1) only those who are ordained may serve as a presiding minister; and (2) at the Holy Communion, the presiding minister serves in the place of Christ, repeating the words and actions of Christ when the Lord's Supper was instituted in the Upper Room. As a result, the presiding minister will be vested a bit differently from the other worship leaders when the Holy Communion is celebrated.

In most parishes, the presiding minister will be wearing an **alb**, a long, white, ankle-length vestment; a **cincture** (SINK-chur), which is a long white rope tied about the waist; and a **stole,** which looks like a very long and narrow, colored scarf worn over the shoulders. The stole is a sign that the wearer has been ordained by the church and is authorized to forgive sins, to preach, to teach, to baptize, and to preside at the Holy Communion.

The presiding minister may also wear a **chasuble** (CHAZ-uh-bul), a colored vestment that looks like a poncho. The chasuble is never worn for any service except the Holy Communion. The chasuble is worn only by the presiding minister, even if other pastors are serving as worship leaders.

On occasion, particularly if a festival is being celebrated, the presiding minister may choose to wear a **cope** during some parts of the service. The cope is a very long and heavy cape. When it is worn, the presiding minister may require the help of the acolyte to get it off and on.

In some parishes, the presiding minister may wear a set of vestments that are different from those listed above. These would include a **cassock,** which is a long, black, ankle-length vestment that is regarded as the basic work clothes for clergy; a **surplice** (SIR-pliss), a long white vestment with full sleeves that evolved from the alb; and a stole.

What the presiding minister wears for the liturgy usually determines the kind of vestments that other worship leaders of the parish will wear.

VESTMENTS FOR THE
ASSISTING MINISTERS

The alb and cincture are usually worn by the musicians, readers, and Communion assistants. However, if the presiding minister is wearing cassock and surplice, the assisting ministers would be vested the same way. Unless an assisting minister is ordained, the stole is not worn.

VESTMENTS FOR THE ACOLYTES

Normally, acolytes would wear whatever vestments are being worn by the other assisting ministers.

Let's face it, acolytes are oftentimes quite uncomfortable when it comes to vestments—and they oftentimes show it, and with good reason! They are frequently asked to wear vestments that are either too big or too small and, when they don't fit, acolytes hate to have to go out in front of all those people.

Even when the vestment fits, it sometimes looks as though someone had used it as a cleaning rag. If they are soiled and wrinkled, if they don't fit well, they are really not appropriate for use at worship.

But there is also another side to this matter: the way some acolytes care for the vestments that are provided. Carefully pressed albs get yanked off their hangers, they are thrown aside if the wrong one was selected, and they sometimes get brutalized and mutilated and abused during hallway sports before the service. By the time the procession forms, some acolyte vestments look as though they are ready to be used as cleaning rags! Acolytes should know better.

It's just as true for acolytes as it is for other worship leaders. To put on a vestment is to put on a special identity, and attitudes and behavior are powerfully affected by that act. In vestments, worship leaders are regarded as servants and instruments of the Holy Spirit. They now have the privilege of helping to awaken in others those thoughts and attitudes which make them want to worship God.

As long as you've got those vestments on—before and during and after the service—people expect a lot of you. They expect you to provide a good example of what it means to worship and how one should worship. As far as they're concerned, you are the model to be followed. Therefore, try to be careful while you are "up there"—lighting candles, walking in procession, moving about the chancel, listening to the readings and the sermon, singing the hymns and the liturgy, receiving Communion—for you are *always* being noticed and you are *always* teaching people about the meaning of worship.

It's for this reason that you are told *not* to yawn or scratch or slouch or chew gum or wave at friends or play with your cincture or explore your nose or look bored or flirt or visit or act as though you wished that you were somewhere else.

As a worship leader, as one who desires to let people see something of the glory and majesty of God, let a sense of reverence control you as you carefully put on your vestments and begin your tasks. Those vestments make it very clear that you are now an active agent of the Holy Spirit, sharing in the church's primary mission: the proclamation and celebration of the Gospel of Jesus Christ.

5
What
Do
Acolytes Do ?

Acolytes are worship leaders. While they usually do not have any speaking assignments during the liturgy, theirs is yet a ministry of proclamation and celebration. Those acolytes who see themselves only as decorations for the service and as luxury items that the church could easily do without are either missing the point of their ministry or the parish is making poor use of them. To have an effective ministry, acolytes must understand that the church expects them to do three things at worship: (1) to worship, (2) to enable the congregation to worship, (3) to enable other worship leaders to do their tasks well.

ACOLYTES AS WORSHIPERS

Acolytes are, first of all, worshipers. With other baptized members of the family of God, they have come to church to do what Christians like most to do: gather with other believers in the high and holy act of thanking and praising God. Acolytes are not stagehands or pieces of scenery or spectators; they are worshipers who come to the liturgy of Word and Meal to be caught up in the electric drama of conversation with God and all the saints.

Therefore, acolytes will sing when the congregation sings. They will pray and watch and listen and commune along with the other worshipers. Their worship books are open to the proper page. They will sit and stand and kneel and bow and make the sign of the cross along with everyone else at worship. After all, acolytes are worship leaders; their effectiveness as leaders is related to their full involvement as worshipers.

ACOLYTES AS WORSHIP LEADERS

As worship leaders, acolytes understand that they are to help enable and encourage those in attendance to worship. Acolytes, knowing that

God is present, will seek to make that Presence known and obvious to all worshipers. Their every action and motion will be one of devotion and reverence. They know that some of the people present may not live beyond the week. Some may be there for the very first time. Some of those present still do not know what worship is all about. Some who are present sincerely love Christ and Christ's church and are expecting a full and enriching liturgy.

Therefore, as worship leaders acolytes will attempt to serve the expectations and needs of all the various kinds of people who are in attendance. For sure, they won't act the fool. They won't act as though worship has no importance. They won't act bored or indifferent, nor will they do their tasks carelessly. Because they have prayed and prepared and practiced, the acolytes will serve with reverence, calmness, and genuine hospitality. Because of such caring, all present will gain a keener vision of the majesty and glory of God.

ACOLYTES AS PART OF A TEAM

The presiding minister, the musicians, readers, the Communion assistants, and the ushers all work in partnership with the acolytes. As worship leaders, you are all linked together as a kind of team. Each worship leader has to assume that every other worship leader knows what is happening during each part of the service and also knows what is to happen next. Because each service has been carefully planned and rehearsed, each part of the liturgy is done with naturalness. The presiding minister doesn't have to be told when to lift the bread. The lector doesn't have to be pushed into place to read the lessons. The organist doesn't have to be told how many stanzas are in the hymn. The ushers don't have to be reminded that it's time to bring the offerings to the altar. Nor does the acolyte have to be elbowed to light the Advent wreath. Careful planning and careful rehearsals have made all that sort of thing unnecessary.

While worship is a holy activity, it is something done by humans; therefore, errors can and do happen. After all, only God is perfect! Worship leaders, being human, do get confused and forgetful once in a while and need a quiet signal to get them back on track. That's perfectly understandable. However, worship leaders should not use their humanity as an excuse for poor planning and lazy preparation. Because so much depends upon that special time with God, and because worship leaders want so much to be useful agents of the Holy Spirit, they will work together so that the congregation has a better chance to discover and experience true and fulfilling worship.

With this understanding of worship leadership, the details of the acolytes' tasks can now be considered—even such basic things as walking and sitting. While we do such things every day, it is necessary to remember that there is a liturgical way of sitting and standing and walking. The liturgical way of doing such things may be quite different from the way we sit while watching TV or the way we walk in a shopping mall.

The church has been doing liturgy for thousands of years. Much has been learned about worship and about worshipers during that time. Those accumulated learnings are called *tradition* and they cover a wide range of liturgical matters including such things as posture for worship leaders, lighting the altar candles, who walks where in a procession, what color vestments are used during Lent. These traditions have been shaped by learnings and experiences, and the church has found them to be worth continuing. Having a deep love for God and a high respect for tradition makes it a joy to be a worship leader.

SOME GENERAL INSTRUCTION

Posture

When **standing,** stand straight and tall with head raised and shoulders back. Remember that standing is a symbol of the resurrection, for it is the posture of the living.

When **seated,** sit up straight and tall with head raised and with both feet flat on the floor. Remember that legs are never crossed when one is wearing vestments. That's right: never. Also remember that each hand is placed on each knee when seated, unless a book is being held or the sign of the cross is being made. Arms do not rest on the back of the chair; arms are used to keep hands where they belong.

When **kneeling,** rest upon both knees, keeping your back straight and your head bowed. Kneel; don't squat. Kneel; don't turn yourself into a pretzel.

When **walking,** do so somewhat slowly, with grace and poise. Walk erect with head raised. If you are to carry a cross or candle, it is necessary to keep each of them straight. If you walk and have nothing to carry, your hands should be clasped together above, never below, the waist.

When **bowing,** there are two different forms to be considered. One form of bowing is simply nodding the head slowly. We do that when the processional cross passes, when we approach and pass in front of the altar, and when we receive something from or hand something to another worship leader. This form of bowing is understood to be a simple act of liturgical courtesy.

The other form of bowing is called the **profound bow.** We do that by bending forward from the waist, slowly, gracefully, naturally. The pastor will tell you when this form of bowing is used.

The Hands

The hands are never left to dangle uselessly at our sides or to hold up our chins or to scratch or to be picked at.

The liturgy has needs for our hands: to carry things, to turn pages, to make the sign of the cross, to receive Holy Communion, and to pray. If we are walking and have nothing to carry, our hands are held together just above the waist. If we are seated and have no book to use, our hands are either folded in our lap or placed on our knees.

The Sign of the Cross

During the liturgy, there are several times when we may recall our Baptism by tracing upon ourselves the sign of the cross. This is one of the most ancient acts of devotion that we have in the church. It is one of those liturgical actions that Martin Luther asked us to preserve and use. Luther's Small Catechism says we should make the sign of the cross when we begin and end each day. It helps us remember who and whose we are. It's a clear signal to all that we are baptized and are pleased to make that fact known.

When we make the sign of the cross, the three middle fingers of our right hand are raised to touch the forehead, then lowered to touch the chest, then over to touch the left shoulder, then the right shoulder, and finally to touch the chest again. This act of devotion, tracing the form of our most important symbol, should be done thoughtfully and prayerfully and without haste.

Lighting the Candles

Since this is one of your basic assignments as an acolyte, this section needs to be studied carefully.

Altar candles are lighted for each service and extinguished following each service. Altar candles are lighted by acolytes in vestments and are extinguished by acolytes in vestments, even when no one is around to watch. Such candles remind us that Jesus is the Light of the World. They have been blessed for that purpose. Acolytes have a strong sense of caring for those candles, lighting and extinguishing them with reverence. It requires skill and training to deal with altar candles so that the flame of the candlelighter can easily reach and ignite the wick and that the candles can be extinguished without pushing the wick down into the hot wax where it becomes difficult to light for the next service. There is skill in knowing how to use the bell-shaped snuffer so that it extinguishes the flame by robbing it of oxygen without disturbing the wick.

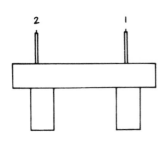

There's an order to be followed when lighting and extinguishing the altar candles. It helps to remember that the candle or candles on the Gospel side (the left side of the altar as you stand in front of it) of the altar never burn alone. That is, other candles are lighted first and extinguished last.

1. Be vested and ready to light the candles when the presiding minister directs.

2. Check the taper in the candlelighter, being sure that it is long enough to light all of the candles.

3. Extend the taper at least an inch, then light it and walk slowly to the altar. As you walk, holding the candlelighter before you, keep your eye on the lighted taper. A sudden draft may threaten it. If the flame goes out, act as though it was supposed to and return to relight the taper.

4. Pause in front of the altar, bow toward it, and then walk to the Epistle side to light the candle there. If you have more than one candle to light there, begin at the candle nearest the center of the altar and work toward the right end of the altar.

5. Then walk back to the center of the altar, bow again, and then walk to the Gospel side to light the candle there. Again, if you have more than one candle to light there, begin at the candle nearest the center of the altar and work toward the left end of the altar.

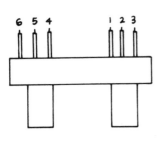

6. Return to the middle of the altar. Look to see that the candles are lit. If not, a wick may be down. That being the case, draw the taper trigger down until the flame goes out. Extend the extinguished taper about two inches, bend the taper down slightly, relight the taper from one of the burning candles, and take the flame to the candle that still needs to be lighted. If the wick refuses to be ignited, act as though it was planned that way and return to the sacristy.

7. Before you leave the altar, extinguish the taper by drawing down the taper trigger slowly and carefully so soot will not fall on the fair

linen. Then bow again toward the altar and return to the sacristy, holding the candlelighter before you as though it were a work of art.

For some services, you may have additional candles to light. If so, don't extinguish the taper at the altar until those other candles have been lighted. Again, take care of the candles on the right side of the chancel first, then on the left. After all the candles have been lighted, walk before the altar, bow toward it, and return slowly to the sacristy.

Extinguishing the Candles

• It's simple. All the candles are extinguished in the reverse order from the way they were lighted. That means, go first to the candles on the Gospel side of the altar, start at the candle nearest the end of the altar and work toward the center. Go to the right side of the altar— bowing toward the altar when you reach the middle of the altar, of course—then extinguish the candles there, starting at the very end of the altar and working toward the center.

• It's not so simple. That bell-shaped snuffer can really make a mess at the altar if you are not very careful. This means that you need to work slowly, holding the snuffer over the flame until it dies from lack of oxygen. If that snuffer hits anything during this action, it probably means that you have gone too far. As a result, the bell-snuffer is sent from the candle with a load of black wax, the candle swallows the wick, bits of soot fall upon the fair linen, and no one will be able to light that candle again until its wick has been repaired.

Lighting the Advent Wreath

During the four weeks before Christmas, many churches place in the chancel a wreath of greens that holds four candles—one for each of the Sundays in Advent. On the First Sunday in Advent, one candle in that wreath is lighted. On the Second Sunday in Advent, two of those candles are lighted. A third candle is lighted on the Third Sunday and all four are lighted on the Fourth Sunday in Advent.

• First Sunday in Advent. During the Psalm, which follows the reading of the First Lesson, take the candlelighter to the altar. Before the altar, bow, then walk to the Gospel side of the altar. With the taper extended about an inch, light it from one of the candles on the Gospel side. Bow again at the center of the altar as you carry the lighted taper to the Advent wreath. Light the first candle on the wreath. After you have determined that the candle is indeed lighted, extinguish the taper and return to your chair.

• Second Sunday in Advent. Before the service, after you light all the altar candles and other candles that may be in the chancel, go to the Advent wreath. At the wreath, light the first candle only. Then, during the Psalm, follow the directions given in the paragraph above, lighting the second candle on the Advent wreath.

• Third Sunday in Advent. Before the service, as all the candles are being lighted, go last to the Advent wreath and light the first and second candles. During the Psalm, light the third candle on the wreath.

• Fourth Sunday in Advent. Before the service, as all the candles are being lighted, go last to the Advent wreath and light the first, second, and third candles. During the Psalm, light the fourth candle on the wreath.

The candles on the Advent wreath will be the first to be extinguished at the conclusion of the liturgy.

Lighting the Paschal Candle

The paschal (PASS-kul) candle is the largest and most decorated candle in the church. Even the stand that holds the paschal candle is tall and is, therefore, sometimes a challenge to get lighted. But it is a candle that needs to be tall; it needs to remind people of a pillar, the kind of pillar of fire that the Israelites followed to find their way from slavery in Egypt to the Promised Land. For us, the paschal candle is a symbol of our Baptism and our escape from the slavery of sin to the new life in Christ. That candle, therefore, is very special to Christians and it is lighted at very special times:

• The Vigil of Easter. During this service, the paschal candle is blessed, given special markings, lighted for the first time, and carried in procession as a sign of Jesus' resurrection from the dead. At this most dramatic service, it is the presiding minister who lights this candle and it is the deacon who carries it.

• The Easter Season. Following the Easter Vigil, the paschal candle is placed in the chancel, near the Gospel side of the altar. It is lighted for every service during the weeks following Easter Sunday. At such services, the paschal candle is usually lighted before the worshipers arrive and is extinguished after the worshipers leave. On the Day of

Pentecost, when the Easter season concludes, the paschal candle is moved from the chancel to the baptistery at the end of the final service that day.

• Holy Baptism. On those days when Holy Baptism is celebrated, the paschal candle is lighted because our Baptism marks our new and eternal life with the resurrected Lord. The paschal candle is lighted after all other candles have been lighted.

• Burial of the Dead. At funerals, the lighted paschal candle may be carried in procession and placed in its stand at the head of the coffin. The paschal candle is not carried outside the church when the coffin is taken away for burial; for such processions, the processional cross is used.

• Aisle Candles. At some services, particularly during the Christmas season, some churches place candles in the aisles. These candles are lighted after all the candles in the chancel have been lighted. They are extinguished before all other candles are extinguished.

Using Two Acolytes as Candle Lighters

In some churches, it may be necessary to use two acolytes to light the candles. If this is the case, the two acolytes, each carrying a lighted candlelighter, stand together before the altar, bow toward it, and light the candles simultaneously.

6
Which
Acolyte
Does What ?

Being an acolyte may mean that you will have several different assignments in the liturgy. Lighting candles may be the basic assignment, but there can be many more. Many of these other assignments have special titles; a good acolyte needs to know these titles and the assignments that are given to each.

This chapter will list and describe the several titles and assignments that may be given to acolytes. Not all acolytes will be expected to do everything described here. You may never be asked to serve as a torchbearer or a bannerbearer. You may never be asked to carry the incense boat. In some parishes, such special assignments may be reserved for those acolytes who have been serving long and well. In some parishes, such assignments may never be given to anyone.

An acolyte at some services may have more than one assignment. It is possible that an acolyte may be asked to light the candles, be a bookbearer, and help prepare the altar for Holy Communion—all at one service! All acolytes need to remember that the more they know the more useful they are to the pastor, to the other worship leaders, and to all the worshipers.

SERVER

Acolytes are called servers when they assist the presiding minister and assisting minister at the altar. Servers would usually be expected to perform the following tasks during the liturgy:

1. Following the Prayers and the Peace, the server goes to the credence table and the assisting minister goes to the altar. The server carries the sacramental vessels and linens one at a time from the

credence, handing each item to the assisting minister in this order:

corporal

purificators

chalice, with a purificator, paten, and pall

host box (if Communion wafers are used)

2. During the Offertory, the server goes before the altar to receive the offering plates from the ushers. With the plates in hand, the server turns toward the altar, raises the plates slightly in an act of presentation, then turns to place the offering plates on the credence table while the bread and wine are presented to the assisting minister at the altar by representatives of the congregation.

3. If a second chalice is needed for the distribution, the server takes it from the credence table—after the ministers have communed—and hands it to the assisting minister who fills it with wine. If Communion trays are used, the server carries one to the communicants at the altar rail, offering each an empty Communion glass. The presiding minister follows the server, giving each communicant the Body of Christ. With a pouring chalice, the assisting minister follows, giving each communicant the Blood of Christ. The used Communion glasses may be collected by another server as each communicant leaves the altar rail.

4. After all have communed, the server stands ready to receive the sacramental vessels and linens from the assisting minister and to place each item on the credence table.

5. When the service is over, the server assists with cleanup as requested.

CRUCIFER

The acolyte who carries the processional cross is called the crucifer. Because such crosses are usually very tall and may be top-heavy, the crucifer needs to be strong and able to handle such an awkward item. During processions, it is often necessary to carry that cross through doorways, under low ceilings, into narrow aisles, up and down steps, around light fixtures, and yet to hold it high so that all can see it.

To carry the processional cross is to give a signal to all the worshipers that Christ is about to enter their company in a very special way and for

a very special reason. It is a great honor to serve as the crucifer, for the crucifer stirs the people to give honor to the cross of Christ.

In most processions the cross goes first as a sign that all Christians follow wherever the cross of Christ leads them. Because the cross is so important to us, candles may be carried beside it to illuminate it and to draw attention to it. Those acolytes who carry those processional torches are called torchbearers. The crucifer and the torchbearers become a special kind of team when the procession forms; they serve as a single unit. A description of a torchbearer follows (see pages 43–45).

1. Before the service begins, the crucifer needs to see that the processional cross is at hand and that the stand for the processional cross is in place in the chancel. While the crucifer waits for the procession to form, great care will be taken so that the cross doesn't get knocked over or used for any horseplay.

2. When it is time to form the procession, the crucifer stands at the head of the procession holding the cross; the torchbearers stand at the sides of the cross.

3. When the signal is given, the crucifer lifts the cross high above all heads, holding it firmly with both hands so that it is carried straight and tall and high. As the procession enters the nave, all worshipers turn to face it, bowing their heads toward the cross in adoration and honor as it passes them in the aisle. As the procession moves into the nave, all are reminded that this is a picture of the Christian life—we're all in a procession, following the cross through life toward heaven.

4. At the altar, the crucifer and torchbearers stop. Without bowing toward the altar, they turn to face the people as the other persons in the procession approach the altar, bow toward the cross, and go to stand at their assigned places. When the presiding minister approaches the altar, all know that the procession has ended for, as Christ's representative in the liturgy, the presider always walks last. The arrival of the presiding

minister serves as a signal for the crucifer and torchbearers to place the processional cross and torches in their stands and then to go to their assigned places during the liturgy.

5. Though it is rare, there may be some services at which a processional cross is used during a *Gospel procession,* especially if the liturgy is being celebrated in a very large space and the cross is needed to mark and identify the place where the Gospel is being read. If that is the case, the crucifer may be expected to do the following:

a. After the Second Lesson has been read, the processional cross and two processional torches are carried before the altar. Crucifer and torchbearers face the altar while the bookbearer and Gospel reader form into procession.

b. As the Verse is being sung, the crucifer leads the Gospel procession into the center aisle. All the people turn to face the cross and the book.

c. When the procession arrives at the place for the reading of the Gospel, the crucifer stands in place facing toward the altar. The torchbearers turn to face each other while the bookbearer stands between them and turns to face toward the altar, holding the book for the Gospel reader.

d. When the reading of the Gospel concludes, the bookbearer and Gospel reader stand aside while the crucifer walks between the torchbearers toward the altar. The torchbearers follow the crucifer, then comes the bookbearer and, at the last, the Gospel reader.

e. The cross and torches are placed in their stands and all go to their assigned places.

6. When the service ends, and a procession out is to be included, the crucifer and torchbearers take cross and torches and lead the procession out of the nave. The order for the procession out is the same as the order for the procession when it entered.

7. Before they remove their vestments, crucifer and torchbearers place the cross and torches in their stands.

TORCHBEARERS

Maybe they don't look much like torches, but that's what the church calls processional candles. Unlike most other candles used at worship, these are mounted on long staffs and are moved from place to place as needed. These torches may be used for any of the many processions that the church will have during the year, and it is the acolytes' job and joy to carry them.

Torches are used to remind people that Christ has come to destroy darkness and to bring light. Torches are also used to draw the attention of the people to an item or to something that is happening. In most processions, the torches accompany and give honor and illumination to the great cross. In a Gospel procession, they give light and honor to the holy book.

Torches are not easily carried. They tend to be a bit top-heavy, they must be carried very straight or hot wax will spill, and they are usually awkward to handle. It requires skill and patience and lots of practice to be a torchbearer.

Since the torchbearers work very closely with the crucifer, the directions for the acolyte who serves as a crucifer need to be studied carefully by each torchbearer. Here are some additional suggestions for torchbearers:

1. Before the procession forms, be sure that the torches and matches are at hand.

2. As the procession forms, see that someone lights each torch. When lighted, each torch must be handled very carefully. No fooling around now. The flame on that torch can burn someone, or it can start a fire, and the hot wax can also burn and can damage vestments, furniture, clothing, and floors. Any acolyte not able to be so cautious is probably not yet ready to be a torchbearer.

3. Torchbearers walk on each side of the crucifer. The torches are held at the same height by all torchbearers. It is the crucifer who determines the walking speed of the procession.

4. When the crucifer reaches the altar and turns to face the people, the torchbearers also face the people by turning in the direction of the cross. When turning at any time during the service, torchbearers never have their backs toward the processional cross.

5. When the procession ends, the torchbearers need to know how to return the torches to their stands without tilting the torches and without making a lot of noise. The torches do fit their stands and only practice, practice, practice can give torchbearers the skills they need to remove and replace them.

6. Unexpected gusts of wind can easily rob a torch of its flame. Unless a match is nearby and the torch relighted without a lot of confusion, it may be necessary to go without a flame. Don't try to light one torch with another and don't try to light it with one of the altar candles. It's better to act as though the torch was supposed to be out for that part of the service than to go through a lot of waxy gymnastics.

7. During a Gospel procession, as described on page 43, the torchbearers stand on the two sides of the book, facing each other across the book with the torches held at the same height. While the main reason for being there is to honor the book of the Gospel, the torches should be held at a height that enables the reader to see clearly the words that are to be read.

After the Gospel has been read, the bookbearer and the reader step to the side. The crucifer passes between the torchbearers, who then walk with the crucifer toward the altar. The bookbearer follows the torchbearers; the reader follows the bookbearer.

8. When the crucifer walks to the processional cross stand at the end of the service, that is the signal for the torchbearers to walk to the torch stands. As the crucifer lifts the cross from its stand, the torches are also lifted and the torchbearers walk with the crucifer in the procession out of the chancel and nave.

9. The torches are extinguished when the procession ends in the narthex or the sacristy. They are extinguished carefully, either by an acolyte using the bell-snuffer or by the torchbearer, who cups the hand behind the flame and gently blows out the flame. Even after the flame is out, the hot wax remains and is easily spilled. This makes it necessary to hold the torch straight and to handle it carefully as it is restored to its stand.

If, through chance, wax was spilled upon your vestment, let the altar guild know about it before it gets put in the laundry.

BOOKBEARER

The acolyte who carries the lectionary or Gospel book or altar book in the procession is called the bookbearer. Sometimes three books are carried in procession: the altar book, which contains the words and music and prayers of the liturgy; the lectionary, which contains the readings from the Bible that are assigned for each Sunday and holy day of the church year; and the Gospel book, which contains the first four books of the New Testament. Sometimes a bookbearer carries a richly bound Bible to be placed in the pulpit and used during the Gospel procession.

All of these books are important to us as Christians and the bookbearer handles them with care. All three of them contain words that we treasure—they are from the Word of God.

When carried in procession or during the liturgy, these books are held in a special way. Both hands are used, carrying the book as though it were a banner. The book is grasped near the bottom corners, with the spine of the book in the left hand. The book is held in a raised position, making it obvious to all that here is a book of great importance to us all. If the bookbearer is expected to carry a large and heavy edition of the Bible, it may be necessary to have an acolyte with large hands and good muscles.

Certainly no acolyte should be asked to carry a skimpy, paperback, meager-looking edition of any book in procession or use such a book for any part of the liturgy. It's difficult for such books to look as though they are really important.

Let's review the assignments for bookbearers:

1. The book to be carried will have its pages marked with ribbons. These ribbons may be extending from the bottom of the book or from its sides; these ribbons must not be moved or disturbed.

2. Before the procession forms, be sure that the book to be carried is at hand.

3. As the procession forms, stand in your assigned place, holding the book as described above. Make sure that you are about two yards behind the person who walks in front of you during the procession.

4. Before the altar, bow toward it as a sign of respect, then carry the book to its place:

The Bible or lectionary is placed where the lessons are read.

The altar book is placed wherever the presiding minister needs it when the procession ends.

5. At some services, the presiding minister may want the bookbearer to hold the altar book for the first part of the liturgy. If this is the case,  stand before the presiding minister, holding the book as though you were a missal stand. Place your hands at the very bottom of the open book; cup your hands slightly to prevent the book from slipping. The angle and height of the book is determined by the presiding minister. The book will be opened and the pages will be turned by the reader.

6. The bookbearer may be expected to place the altar book on the missal stand at the altar. If the book-bearer is expected to open the altar book to a particular page, be sure to learn which page.

7. At some services there may be a Gospel procession. The book-bearer will be expected to do the following:

a. When the torchbearers go from their chairs to get the torches, the bookbearer goes at the same time to get the Bible or lectionary.

b. With the book being held as a banner, follow the torchbearers to the altar, bow toward it, and then enter the center aisle; walk in procession to the place of the reading.

c. At the place of reading, stand between the two torchbearers and turn to face toward the reader.

d. Assist the reader to open the book to the right page and again hold the book as though you were a missal stand.

e. When the reading concludes, the reader will assist in the closing of the book; the bookbearer will then hold it again as a banner.

f. As the torchbearers turn to walk toward the altar, the bookbearer follows them to the chancel and replaces the Bible or lectionary at the pulpit. The bookbearer then returns to the assigned chair.

8. At the conclusion of the liturgy, the crucifer and torchbearers will go to get the processional cross and torches. This is the signal for the bookbearer to get the book, get into formation in the same order as the procession in, and follow the procession from the nave to narthex or sacristy.

9. Before the vestments are removed, be sure to return the book to its proper place.

BANNERBEARER

The acolyte who carries a banner in procession is called the banner-bearer. A banner is a large piece of fabric, hooked on to a tall staff and carried in procession for special services. A design of some kind is usually attached to the fabric.

Banners are awkward things to carry in procession and they always seem to block a view of where to step next. They are often heavy and are seldom easy to handle. Only a strong, experienced, and very patient acolyte should be asked to serve as a bannerbearer.

If a processional banner is used, the bannerbearer will need to know the following:

1. Before the service, be sure to have the banner at hand and also make sure that the banner stand is in the correct place in the nave or chancel.

2. When the procession forms, carry the banner to your assigned place in the procession; the banner is usually placed following the torchbearers and before the bookbearer. Since the banner has to be carried at an angle, allow a lot of room between the banner and the flames of the torches.

3. As the procession moves, the bannerbearer needs to be aware of such hazards as low ceilings, light fixtures, narrow doors and aisles, worshipers, steps, and needs to know how best to arrive safely at the banner stand.

4. Before the altar, bow your head but not the banner, then walk to the banner stand. Walk to your assigned seat after the banner has been placed securely in its stand.

5. When the service concludes and as the crucifer and torchbearers go to get the processional cross and torches, that is your signal to walk to the banner stand. With the banner, walk before the altar, bow, and join the procession in the order assigned—behind the torchbearers.

6. When the procession ends, return the banner to its proper and safe place.

THURIFER

The acolyte who carries the thurible of incense is called the thurifer. For the church, burning incense is a symbol of repentance and prayer, and it is also used to honor certain liturgical items and to honor all worshipers and worship leaders.

For those parishes which make frequent use of incense in their worship, these directions are provided for the thurifer:

1. A pair of tongs is used to hold the charcoal as it is lighted.

2. The burning charcoal is placed in the thurible and allowed to burn for about fifteen minutes before it is needed for the procession.

3. Just before the procession forms, the presiding minister takes three spoonfuls of incense from the incense boat and puts them on the burning charcoal. The thurifer must keep the thurible in motion, swinging it in small arcs, as the procession forms and moves into the nave.

4. When incense is used in the procession, the thurifer walks before the crucifer. If an acolyte serves as the incense boatbearer, that acolyte also walks before the crucifer, just behind the thurifer.

5. As the thurifer walks in procession, the thurible is carried in the right hand and is swung continuously at the thurifer's right side. The thurifer needs always to prevent the thurible from brushing against vestments or furniture or people.

6. The presiding minister decides whether incense will be used when the procession reaches the altar, during the Gospel procession, during the Offertory, during the singing of the Sanctus, and for the procession at the end of the service. For each of these times, the presiding minister will find it necessary to add more incense to the charcoal. At some services, the thurifer may find it necessary to go to the sacristy to replace and light the charcoal.

7. While the thurible is in the chancel, it will be necessary to provide a stand, where it may be suspended by its chain when not in use.

INCENSE BOATBEARER

The acolyte who carries the incense container in the procession and during the liturgy is called the incense boatbearer. An incense boat is shaped very much like a gravy boat, but is much smaller in size. With the grains of incense, the boat also carries a small spoon that is used to scoop out the incense that is put on the burning charcoal.

It is the task of the boatbearer to stay near the thurifer and to make it easy for the presiding minister to reach the incense spoon and to scoop out the incense into the thurible.

It is very clear that there is much for acolytes to do when the parish assembles for worship. Also obvious is the need for acolytes to spend time learning about the things, actions, and meaning of worship. It is very useful for an acolyte to know all the furnishings, vestments, linens, vessels, actions, and rooms that are part of our worship life, to know a little about their history, and to understand how they are used today in the adoration of God and the enrichment of God's people.

All this certainly points to the need for acolytes to rehearse carefully and thoroughly for each service in which they have assignments. But it is equally important that acolytes understand the absolute necessity of prayer in their training, their serving, and in their worship of God. Praying each day, reading the Bible each day, and each day trying to be a good example of what it means to be a baptized Christian—all of these are part of the life of a worship leader.

Then, when it comes time to put on the vestments and to assist the congregation in the worship of God, devotion and reverence will spring naturally and comfortably from a heart that knows and loves God.

7
What
Happens
on Sunday ?

One bright Sunday morning, about two thousand years ago, the believers made the exciting and electrifying discovery that a most unusual miracle had happened. It had happened in a cemetery, of all places; and it had happened at the grave of Jesus. Jesus, who had been cruelly killed on the cross, had been buried in this grave the previous Friday afternoon. That grave, which was really a small cave, had been firmly sealed with a gigantic stone. But now, on Sunday morning, that stone had been mysteriously thrust aside and the dead Jesus had stepped from that grave as the living Christ.

That Sunday morning miracle changed everything, for it proved that every word and promise of Jesus about life and about death was absolutely true. No Sunday since then has ever been the same. For Christians, every Sunday is a celebration of the resurrection of Jesus Christ. Every Sunday we gather as resurrected people to remember with high delight all of the words and acts and promises of our saving God. Every Sunday we recount the birth, ministry, death, resurrection, and ascension of the world's savior. As we recall, recount, and remember these mighty acts of God, we have a keen awareness that God is with us and that we are being drawn into a new and surprising contact with God and all the company of heaven.

That contact happens because our Lord has promised to be with us always, even to the end of the world. Through God's holy Word and through God's holy Meal that presence is proven and, suddenly, God is in action again. In that place, around that altar, through words and songs and prayers and bread and wine and holy acts of thanksgiving, God does for us what we cannot do for ourselves. Sunday is still a day of miracles.

That ancient and yet ever new liturgy of the church sets the stage for those weekly miracles. That liturgy won't let any generation forget the wondrous works of God. That liturgy won't let any of us lose our awareness that God still has things that need to happen to us before we are ready to cope with the grandeur and excitement of heaven.

Acolytes will want to look at the liturgy carefully so that they may grow in their understanding of it, to look at it as persons who have been given the privilege of opening the veil of divine mysteries so that all gain a glimpse of the glory of God. At no time and in no way would acolytes want to delay or to detract from the miracles that God would perform through Word and Meal every Sunday. As worship leaders, acolytes want only to be useful to God, to tell well God's story, to permit the enlightenment and enrichment of God's people, and to offer God their sincere praise and thanksgiving.

At Home

Getting ready for the liturgy begins at home. That includes getting enough sleep so that no one is drowsy or sluggish at church. It also includes careful attention to personal hygiene—hair combed, nails cleaned and trimmed, hands and face washed. Prayer is also an important part of getting ready for the liturgy—thanking God for the new day, for the privilege of being a baptized Christian, and asking God for help so that the liturgy will be celebrated sincerely and reverently.

In the Sacristy

Acolytes should arrive at the church at least twenty minutes before the liturgy begins. They, along with other worship leaders, will quietly go about their tasks as they make final preparations for worship:

books are marked and in place
sacramental vessels and linens are set in place
items to be carried in the procession are at hand
bulletins are on the sedilia
candlewicks have been properly trimmed
matches have been found
vestments have been put on—neatly and correctly

When all is ready, the worship leaders have prayer together, the candles are lighted, and the liturgy begins to the glory of God and for the good of God's people.

Brief Order for
Confession and Forgiveness

Before the entrance hymn is sung, the presiding minister may lead the congregation in an act of preparation, called confession and forgiveness. Notice that the sign of the cross is made when confession begins as a clear reminder that it is Baptism that gives us the courage to admit our wrongs. The sign of the cross is also made as we receive forgiveness—it is our way of showing that we accept this gift of mercy.

The Procession and Entrance Hymn

Many persons can be included in the procession or just a few. It all depends upon the kind of liturgy that is being celebrated—a great festival or a regular kind of Sunday. The congregation sings the Entrance Hymn as the procession enters the nave and the worship leaders take their places in the chancel.

CRUCIFER

TORCHBEARER   **TORCHBEARER**

BOOKBEARER

ASSISTING MINISTER

PRESIDING MINISTER

Apostolic Greeting

The presiding minister, using words from the Bible, greets the congregation in God's Name. As the greeting is spoken, all turn toward the presiding minister and bow their heads, showing that the greeting is accepted. The response is spoken, never mumbled, with all standing erectly, speaking directly to the presiding minister.

Kyrie and Hymn of Praise

One or both or neither of these may be sung, depending upon the season of the church year.

Salutation and Prayer of the Day

Many prayers begin with an exchange of greeting between the presiding minister and the congregation. All turn toward the presiding minister and bow during the words "The Lord be with you." The response, "And also with you," is directed to the presiding minister. The "Amen" at the end of the prayer should be spoken with firmness.

The First Lesson

All eyes and heads are turned toward the reader. All give close attention to the reading of these words from the Bible; they have been carefully chosen to help us understand what today's liturgy is emphasizing. This first reading is usually from the Old Testament.

Psalm

This song, from the church's oldest hymnal, was chosen because it fits well with the day's assigned Bible readings.

The Second Lesson

This second reading is usually from one of the epistles (letters) in the New Testament. Again, be sure to give your eyes and ears to the reader of these holy words.

The Verse

This brief song gets everybody on their feet for it prepares us for the reading of the liturgy's chief lesson, the Holy Gospel. The Verse serves as a processional hymn for the one who goes to the place where the Gospel will be announced and read.

The Holy Gospel

A reading from one of the first four books of the New Testament is greeted and concluded with liturgical cheers. Again, all eyes and ears are directed toward the reader as the Good News of the Gospel is read.

The Sermon

The pastor, because of training and ordination, helps all to understand what the readings have to do with the Christian's life and work today. We give attention to every word—they tell us what we need to know as we try to live out the will of God.

Silence

Following the Sermon, the congregation is given time to give careful thought to what has been read and sung and preached. No one fidgets or stirs or turns pages in the worship book; silence also means to be physically still.

Hymn of the Day

This hymn, seen as the most important of the service, has been carefully chosen so that it continues the message of the readings and the Sermon. For this hymn, all stand.

The Creed

Either the Apostles' or Nicene Creed is used. It's the church's bold and enduring statement about the Christians' belief and allegiance. All heads are held high and all voices are firm and convincing as the Creed is confessed.

The Prayers

Because of Baptism, Christians dare to call upon Almighty God to get immediately and directly involved in the many problems that face everybody in the world. We pray for the church, the nations of the world, bishops and other leaders, for peace, for the sick and dying, and in thanksgiving for all the blessed dead.

The Peace

Now the first part of the liturgy ends. The exchange of the sign of peace is the bridge to the liturgy of the Eucharistic Meal, that special moment when in love, Christians turn toward one another. Through handclasp or embrace or kiss, we let the peace of the Lord draw us together into one united, dedicated family of peacemakers.

The Offering

As the gifts of money are gathered, worship leaders prepare the altar for the celebration of the liturgy of the Upper Room. The vessels and linens are reverently brought to the holy table in preparation for the holy Meal.

Offertory

This song is another processional hymn for those who now bring the gifts of money, bread, and wine to the altar. These gifts of money will be used to spread the Gospel to the world; the bread is offered as a sign of human toil, and the wine is offered as a sign of the joys we know as the people of God.

The Offertory Prayer

The gifts have been presented at the altar and through this prayer the congregation offers these gifts to God. Following this prayer the presiding minister goes to the altar to stand in the footprints of Jesus to repeat the words and actions of Jesus in the Upper Room.

NOTE: A different kind of energy now overtakes the liturgy as it leads us to remember and confront the events of Holy Week. It's time to recall our Lord's journey to the cross and grave.

Preface and Proper Preface

Thanksgiving is the key word as we begin this part of the liturgy. The liturgy reminds us that heaven is so involved in our worship that angels and archangels and all the company of heaven crowd into our church to join us in the praise of God.

Holy, Holy, Holy

Through the liturgy, the first Palm Sunday is recalled as we sing the same song of welcome that the people of Jerusalem sang as Jesus entered that holy city. For Christians this is understandably a very moving song, for we remember that Jesus wept in sadness as he heard the people cheer him for the wrong reasons. It is meaningful and proper to bow during the singing of the first half of this song and to make the sign of the cross as we sing, "Blessed is he who comes in the name of the Lord."

Eucharistic Prayer

From the streets of Jerusalem, the liturgy at last places us in the Upper Room. The presiding minister, serving in the place of Jesus, now repeats the words and actions of the Lord's Supper. When Jesus took the bread and wine, he gave thanks. For that reason, the Words of Institution are set within a prayer of thanksgiving.

For all Christians, this is a very special time in the liturgy. Bread and wine are being blessed, to be for us the true Body and Blood of Jesus. Christ comes to us, offering each of us his life, his person, his love, and his grace. Reverence is our response to this holy mystery.

The Communion

As we sing "Lamb of God," thoughts of Good Friday come to mind, the day Jesus' Body was broken and Blood was shed on the cross for the sins of the world. But as we approach the altar to receive Holy Communion it is suddenly Easter, for there we are offered the resurrected and living Christ.

To receive the Body of our Lord, we first make the sign of the cross and then we make a throne for him with our hands: palms up, the right hand resting in the left, the arms extended as the presiding minister gives us the bread. Then, both hands are brought to the mouth and the bread is eaten reverently. After receiving the bread, bow the head and quietly say "Amen."

To receive the Blood of our Lord, grasp the base of the chalice to assist the minister as the cup is put to your lips. Bow the head after receiving the wine, and quietly say "Amen" as you make the sign of the cross.

When you return to your place from the altar, bow or kneel in prayer, thanking God that you and others have been given such a precious gift: oneness with Christ and nourishment to live out your Baptism. As others receive Communion, sing the hymns and offer silent prayers of thanksgiving that God continues to visit us with healing and hope.

Post-Communion

Following the Communion, the liturgy draws quickly to an end. We give thanks through song, prayer, and a time of silence. And, finally, in the name of God, the presiding minister blesses us. For that blessing, all heads are bowed and all may make the sign of the cross as a sign that we gladly accept that blessing as we face the days before us. Then, the assisting minister speaks the words of dismissal and, with a shouted "Thanks be to God," the congregation scatters to bring Christ's presence to a waiting world.

The Church Year

Christians have a special calendar. It's called the *church year* or the *liturgical year.* This calendar doesn't have months, but it does have seasons and it does have days that are so special we call them *holy days.*

The Christian calendar has six seasons. The first five of those seasons are all about Jesus: his birth, his suffering and death, and his resurrection. These first five seasons find us giving attention to the events in the life of Jesus, events that brought about our forgiveness and salvation.

The sixth season of the liturgical year is the longest of them all—up to twenty-eight weeks. This season is also about Jesus, but now our attention is on his teachings, his miracles, his sermons. Therefore, the Christian year has two halves: the first half (the first five seasons) celebrates his life's story; the second half (the long sixth season) celebrates the truths that Jesus came to give us.

The Christian calendar also has some special days included. Some of those special days mark unusual events in the life of the church, such as the Day of Pentecost and the Conversion of Saint Paul. But most of these special days are celebrated in remembrance of the apostles, martyrs, teachers, missionaries, and other servants of God who lived and died for the Christian faith.

Every liturgy that we celebrate is affected by the seasons and holy days of the church year. That church year determines which parts of the Bible we will hear every week as we worship, as well as the color of the vestments and paraments that are used, the hymns we will sing, and whether certain additional candles are to be lighted. All of these things help keep our attention on that which the church knows to be important for our growth in faith and usefulness as baptized Christians.

In the church's worship book can be found a full list of the seasons and holy days of the liturgical year. That list also shows the liturgical color that is assigned to each season and holy day. Acolytes will find it interesting and useful to be acquainted with the Christian's calendar.

The Seasons of the
First Half of the Church Year

Advent—we prepare to celebrate the coming of the Savior

Christmas—we celebrate the birth of our Savior, Jesus

Epiphany (ee-PIFF-ah-nee)—we celebrate the revelation that Jesus is God's Son

Lent—we prepare to celebrate the death and resurrection of Jesus and to renew our baptismal commitment

Easter—we celebrate the resurrection of Jesus

The Second Half of the Church Year

The Season after Pentecost

Prayers for Acolytes

In the Morning

Make the sign of the cross in remembrance of your Baptism, saying:
In the Name of the Father, and of the Son, and of the Holy Spirit. Amen.

I give thanks to you, heavenly Father, through Jesus Christ, your dear Son, that you have protected me through the night from all danger and harm; and I ask you to preserve and keep me this day also from all sin and evil; that in all my thoughts, words, and deeds I may serve and please you. Into your hands I commend my body and soul, and all that is mine. Let your holy angel have charge over me, that the wicked one have no power over me. Amen.

—From Luther's Small Catechism (revised)

Before Worship

Bless ✝ me, O God, with a reverent sense of your presence, that I may be at peace and may worship you with all my mind and spirit; through Jesus Christ, our Lord. Amen.

Before Holy Communion

O Jesus, our great high priest, be present with us as you were present with your disciples, and make yourself known to us in the breaking of the bread. Amen.

After Holy Communion

Preserve in us, O Jesus, the gift of your grace, that, by the power and strength of the Eucharist which we have received, we may be armed against all evils now and forever. Amen.

At Bedtime

Trusting in the gifts of Baptism, make the sign of the cross, saying:
In the Name of the Father, and of the Son, and of the Holy Spirit. Amen.

I give thanks to you, heavenly Father, through Jesus Christ your dear Son, that you have this day so graciously protected me, and I ask you to forgive me all my sins, and the wrong which I have done, and by your great mercy defend me from all the perils and dangers of this night. Into your hands I commend my body and soul, and all that is mine. Let your holy angel have charge over me, that the wicked one have no power over me. Amen.

—From Luther's Small Catechism (revised)